UNDERSTANDING

TERRAPINS

OTHER TITLES AVAILABLE

UNDERSTANDING TERRAPINS

RUTH MIDGLEY

NIMROD PRESS LTD
15 The Maltings
Turk Street
Alton, Hants

First Edition, 1987

Produced by Ptarmigan Printing

Published by:
NIMROD PRESS LTD
15 The Maltings
Turk Street
Alton, Hampshire
England

CONTENTS

PREFACE AND ACKNOWLEDGMENTS

After keeping and managing Terrapins for a number of years I felt other enthusiasts may be interested in my experiences. This was the basis for writing this guide which it is hoped will be useful for all who wish to be involved with this fascinating creature the Terrapin.

I would like to thank:

> Fishworld Vivarium, Grimsby
>
> Blue Lagoon, Grimsby
>
> Stephen, my brother, who helped with the photographs

Ruth Midgley

Chapter 1

HISTORY

INTRODUCTION

The first reptiles evolved 300-million years ago in the Carboniferous period. It was 190-million years ago that members of the class to which tortoises and turtles belong evolved. This was in the mesozoic era of the Triassic period. It is thought that tortoises and turtles evolved before other reptiles; such as those representative of the snake and crocodilian groups. Also, it is thought that they evolved before dinosaurs.

The order to which the tortoises and turtles belong, is known as the order **Chelonia** or **Testudinata**. This class is split up into two halves as is shown in the diagram (fig.1).

Chelonians have two shells, an upper one called the **carapace** and a lower one called the **plastron**. Besides the shells they have the usual skeletal structure.

DEFINITIONS

As this book is about terrapins it is necessary to understand what is meant by a "terrapin". The first definition is one adhered to by biologists and naturalists. It is, that a terrapin is the name given to the seven geographical races of Malaclemys terrapin, living in the eastern part of N.America. This variety grows up to ten inches in length (carapace measurement), and is known in America as the 'Diamondback'. It is important to say that the Malaclemys terrapin

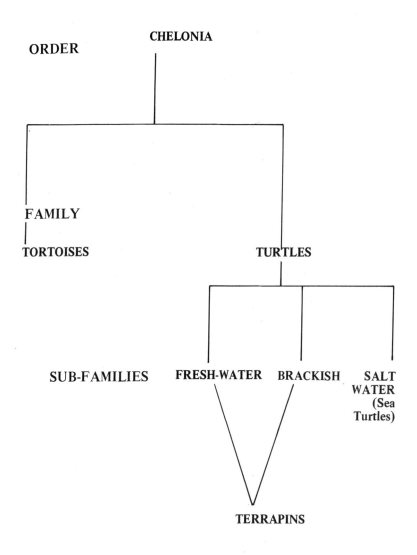

ORDER   CHELONIA

FAMILY

TORTOISES   TURTLES

SUB-FAMILIES   FRESH-WATER   BRACKISH   SALT WATER (Sea Turtles)

TERRAPINS

Figure 1 **Classification Diagram**

lives in the sea, and in salt and brackish water lakes along the Atlantic coast of N.America.

The second definition of a terrapin, is that it is a fresh-water turtle. Since the Malaclemys terrapin lives in brackish and sea-water this is rather misleading. Later on in this introduction I shall illustrate the differences between what I consider to be turtles; and what I consider is a terrapin. The small turtles such as the European pond turtle, the Red-eared or Elegant turtle, Map and Painted turtles also Snapping turtles are all fresh-water varieties. These I consider to be terrapins.

Tortoises and Terrapins

Before I consider the differences between turtles and terrapins, I think it is necessary to illustrate the difference between tortoises and terrapins.

The first main difference lies in the shape of the upper shell. That of a tortoise is highly domed, whereas that of a terrapin is much flatter and gently sloping; thus:

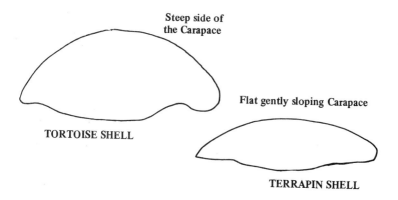

The second main difference concerns the limbs, especially the fore-limbs. The terrapin has a web of skin in between each claw on all four feet, so that it can swim quickly and efficiently. The tortoise does not have webbed feet, and its limbs are thick and clumsy-looking. The claws are thick, horny and short, consequently the tortoise can move only slowly on land. The limbs of a terrapin are longer in proportion to its body, slender and light; therefore it can move quickly, both in an aquatic and terrestrial environment. Thus:

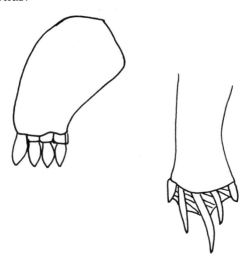

The final most important difference is that tortoises are *vegetarians* whilst terrapins are *carnivorous* feeders.

Turtles and Terrapins

Now I shall describe the differences between terrapins and their larger sea-going relatives.

1. Size

A large terrapin (depending on the variety) may grow up to three feet in length. However, a large sea-turtle (example the Leatherback turtle) may grow up to over eight feet in length and could weigh as much as half a ton.

2. Conformation of the shell.

That of a sea-turtle, (example Hawksbill turtle) is heavier and a far more solid construction than that of a terrapin. This is to withstand the pressure of the water as the turtle swims deeper, turtles have leathery shells also for this reason.

3. Limbs
The limbs of a sea-turtle are modified into flat flippers so that they can swim extremely quickly and efficiently. However, when a turtle comes ashore to lay its eggs, locomotion is very slow and laborious. Sea-turtles spend 95% of their life in the sea, coming ashore only to lay their eggs. Terrapins however spend approximately 50% of their life on land and 50% of it in water.

VARIETIES OF TERRAPINS

Now we are clear what a terrapin is and how it differs from its relatives; we can take a look at different varieties of terrapin which are available for sale in Britain.

1. European Pond Turtle (*Emys orbicularis*)
This terrapin has a dark green carapace with tiny yellow spots radiating over its entire surface. It can measure up to seven inches in length and is ideal for ponds because of its hardiness.

2. Painted Terrapin
There are four types of Painted terrapin. They are divided into: —

(a) Western Painted terrapin   (*Chrysemys   picta   belli*)
(b) Eastern Painted terrapin (*Chrysemys picta picta*)
(c) Midland Painted terrapin (*Chrysemys picta marginata)*
(d) Southern Painted terrapin (*Chrysemys picta dorsalis*)

The difference between the first three varieties is only that the orange markings on the plastron are slightly different. The Southern Painted terrapin is different from the other three varieties; in that it has a bright orange stripe, running from its head-end to its tail-end on its carapace. In all varieties the carapace is a muddy-brown colour.

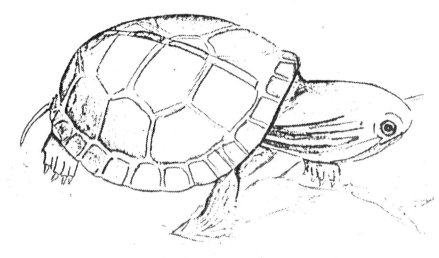

Southern Painted Terrapin

European Pond Terrapin (suitable for ponds)

3. Map terrapin (*Graptemys geographica*)

This terrapin's carapace usually has a pattern on it resembling a map. It is roughly the same size as the Painted terrapins, (to which it is related) which can grow up to eight inches in length in captivity.

4. Red-Eared or Elegant terrapin (*Pseudemys scripta elegans*)

This terrapin is the most popular of all. It has a dark-green carapace with markings in yellow, brown and black. There is an elongated red stripe behind each eye, giving the terrapin its common name. The terrapin can measure up to twelve inches in length in captivity, although these large species are rarely seen.

The following pages are intended to be a comprehensive guide to educate people in caring for these reptiles properly.

Map Terrapin

Chapter 2

HABITAT OF THE TERRAPIN

Many of the imported species of terrapin are native to North America. These **chelonians** are wild and live in and around the lakes, where they are frequently seen basking on rocks and logs in the sun.

North America is one of the warmest countries in the world. For an example, I will quote the temperature and humidity figures for Florida. The temperature in winter is about 80 degrees farhrenheit and rises to 87 degrees in the summer. Compare these figures to the winter and summer temperatures of London, and you will find they are considerably higher. The high temperatures of Florida have the effect of warming the lakes and streams. A combination of heat in the air and warm water gives a hot and humid atmosphere. In fact the humidity figures in winter are 66%, and 68% in summer. The percentages indicate the amount of water droplets in the atmosphere, compared to the air content of it. To generalise more, the example I have given will be similar to the temperature and humidity readings that most varieties of terrapin live in. The weather in North America is more constant than it is here in Britain, but even in the wettest of seasons the temperatures are still high.

WARMTH ESSENTIAL

After reading the last paragraph, what comes over most of all is that terrapins need to live in a warm climate. They invariably live in environments that are constantly warm. This heat factor is most important to all terrapins as it is to other reptiles because they are all POIKILOTHERMS. This word means that reptiles cannot generate their own body temperature. Instead, they have to take in the warmth from around them, and use that to operate all their bodily functions. Without heat or warmth they die. Mammals on the other hand like you or me are HOMIOTHERMS. This means that we can make our own body heat within us by various methods, for our bodies to function. In practical terms what all this means is that if a terrapin is put into cold water it will eventually die.

The above statement is very true. Many of the imported terrapins are bought by people who keep them in shallow bowls of cold water. Having read the first part of this chapter you know that for survival terrapins need warmth, light a good depth of clean water to swim in and an area of dry land. In fact, in setting up a tank suitable for terrapins, it is necessary to try to copy the natural environment of the species that you have. The equipment that is needed to convert a fish tank into an environment suitable for terrapins, is as follows:

1. A medium sized tank
2. **Heater** and **thermostat** to govern temperature
3. **Filter** and **air-pump** to keep the water clean
4. **Light bulbs**
5. Suitable depth of **swimming water**
6. **Dry** area of **land** for the terrapins to bask on
7. **Thermometer** to keep a check on the water's temperature.

These various devices are the bare essentials needed for creating a terrapin-like environment. If you cannot give your terrapins the bare essentials which they need to survive **then it is wrong to keep them.** Before buying a puppy or kitten, we rush to the shops to obtain feeding bowls, baskets, collars and leads for them. Heaters, thermostats and filters are just as important in keeping terrapins. If they cannot be provided, it is cruel to keep these delightful chelonians.

FILTER DRAWINGS

Filters are discussed in the next Chapter. The four types all serve a specific purpose.

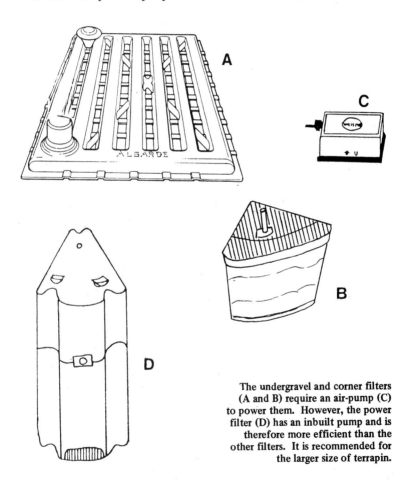

The undergravel and corner filters (A and B) require an air-pump (C) to power them. However, the power filter (D) has an inbuilt pump and is therefore more efficient than the other filters. It is recommended for the larger size of terrapin.

Chapter 3

TANK SET UPS

In Chapter two I described a typical terrapin's habitat and related it to how a tank should be set up. More detail is now given. The following are tank set-ups for small, medium and large terrapins.

SET-UP I

TANK FOR HATCHLINGS
(Carapace measurement up to 2¼ inches)

The requirements are:—
1. A tank which measures 18 x 12 x 12 inches — this will house up to four hatchlings.
2. A combined heater and thermostat unit.
3. One 25 watt light bulb, also a condensation shield and lid to fit the tank.
4. An undergravel filter.
5. An air pump, e.g. **Whisper 400**. This powers the undergravel filter.
6. Thermometer to keep a check on the water's temperature.
7. One to two inches of swimming water.
8. Flat sided rock for an area of land, also gravel to cover the filter.
9. Console for all the wiring up.

SPECIAL NOTES: The size of the tank mentioned above

will house the terrapins for about a year (when they measure 2¼ inches follow tank set-up Number II). The heat is provided by the combined heater and thermostat unit which should be placed horizontally and completely submerged in the tank. The light bulb also gives off a small amount of heat. Terrapins like to bask on rocks under bulbs. The condensation shield fits into the lid (most lids can be bought with inbuilt shields) and protects the light bulb from being splashed. Terrapins tend to be boisterous and could fuse the bulb if it has no protection from the water. The light should be on all day, i.e., from 8am to 9pm.

CONDENSATION SHIELD

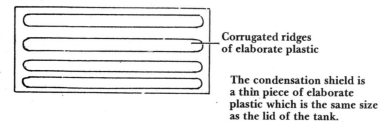

Corrugated ridges
of elaborate plastic

The condensation shield is
a thin piece of elaborate
plastic which is the same size
as the lid of the tank.

UNDERGRAVEL FILTER

The undergravel filter, as its name suggests, has to be placed under a two or three inch layer of fine gravel. It completely covers the bottom of the tank. When you buy an undergravel filter you get the base for the size of tank you have, e.g., 18 x 12 inch. Also enclosed is an air-lift (a plastic cylindrical tube) which fits into the base. As the water level for hatchlings has to be low the air-lift has to be cut so that it measures only 1½ inches in length.

The lift has to be just underneath the water level. An air stone can be put into the lift to give off lots of small bubbles instead of big noisy ones. The tubing fits onto the air stone, comes out of the air lift and the end fits onto the air pump.

PHOTOGRAPH OF AN UNDERGRAVEL FILTER TAKEN FROM ABOVE.

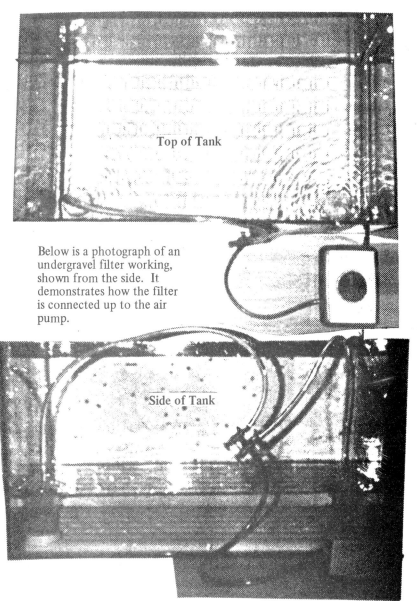

Top of Tank

Below is a photograph of an undergravel filter working, shown from the side. It demonstrates how the filter is connected up to the air pump.

Side of Tank

The thermometer registers the temperature of the water. It should be 80 degrees fahrenheit, however at night you will notice that it drops a few degrees. The depth of water should only be about two inches while the hatchlings are particularly small. Terrapins breathe by lungs not gills like fish, so if the water is deep, with small terrapins there is the risk of them drowning.

About a third of the tank should be convered into land for the terrapins to bask on. Especially when young, the rays in the light emitted by the light bulb is especially important in strengthening the terrapin's shell. For the land a reasonably big, flat sided rock is needed.

As there will be wires leading from the air pump, heating unit and light bulb, it is wise to buy a console. This is a small elongated box with special areas for wires from the different pieces of equipment. A console makes wiring up easy, safe and efficient. Instructions are always enclosed. Always make sure that before doing any wiring up, the mains switch is off. A flex goes from the console to plug in normally.

Picture of a tank designed for hatchlings

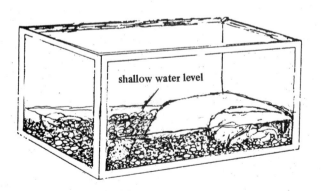

shallow water level

SET-UP II

TANK SUITABLE FOR SMALL TO MEDIUM
SIZED TERRAPINS
(terrapins with a carapace length of 2¼ to 5 inches)

Requirements: —
1. Tank which measures 24 x 12 x 15 inches (houses up to four medium sized terrapins).
2. Separate heater, thermostat and thermometer.
3. Two 25 watt light bulbs, also a condensation shield and lid.
4. Corner filters and air pump, e.g., **Whisper 400**.
5. Rocks and gravel to build an area of land.
6. Swimming water at a depth of two to four inches.
7. Console to house wires.

SPECIAL NOTES: The **Size of tank** mentioned above will house the terrapins until they measure five to six inches in length. There are slight changes between this set up, and the set up for hatchlings. In this set up you need two light bulbs, also the water is slightly deeper; therefore the land you construct has to be built higher. This can be done by using two or three rocks. Gravel should be put into the gaps in between the rocks, to make a strong, stable construction. Make sure the land area is safe otherwise a falling rock could kill a terrapin.

Regarding the **heating unit**, in the larger tanks, it is best to have a separate heater and thermostat, rather than a combined model as in Set-Up one. The reason for this is simply that separate units work far more efficiently in heating up the water, than a combined model does, for this size of tank. The heater should be put at the opposite end of the tank from the thermostat. They should both be slanting upwards, but completely submerged at the back of the tank.

The only other difference is the type of **filter** to use.

Corner filters are best for this size of terrapin. Dirt collects in them and they can be removed, cleaned and replaced easily. Put gravel into the bottom of the corner filter to weight it down. On top of this put a layer of filter medium, then charcoal (to purify the water) and finally a second layer of medium. The number of filters required depends upon the number and size of terrapins you keep.

Opposite is a picture of a corner filter.

The picture below shows a tank suitable for small to medium terrapins.

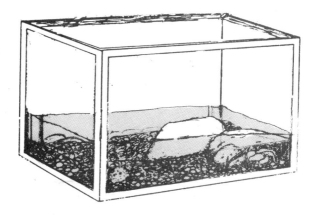

SET-UP III

Tank for large terrapins (with a carapace length of six inches and over).

Requirements:—
1. Tank which measures at least 3ft x 1ft x 15 inches.
2. Two 25 watt light bulbs, condensation shield and lid.
3. Separate heater, thermostat also a thermometer.
4. Power filter; e.g. **Sicce 42** model.
5. Rocks and gravel to build land.
6. Depth of water at least five inches and deeper.
7. Console.

SPECIAL HOMES

The tank needs to be large for these big terrapins, if it is too small, it could stunt their growth. A tank of the size described should house two terrapins up to eight or nine inches in length.

The type of **filter** to use is a power filter, I recommend **Sicce 42** model. As this is a power filter it does not require an air pump. It is only suitable for large terrapins because the jet of water is so powerful it could smash a smaller terrapin onto a rock. A powerful filter is needed to cope with the increasing amount of detrimental matter, this is a problem when keeping large terrapins. The filter works best

Picture of the Sicce 42 power filter

completely submerged in water, laid on its side. It does not need carbon (charcoal), it has its own triangular shaped sponge to trap the dirt. This needs replacing with a new one every few months. Cleaned once a week, the power filter is the quickest filter to clean. I call it the 'five minute filter', as that is all the time it takes to clean.

The **land** will need to be built higher again as the water is deeper. It may need building up once every two days. Also water will have to be put in the tank every week, to replace that which is lost due to evaporation. For the other pieces of equipment on the list see both tank one and tank two set ups for details.

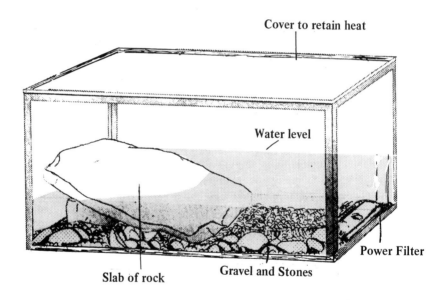

Picture of a tank for large terrapins

These tank set ups are easy to follow and provide the best environments needed for promoting health and growth. If followed carefully the terrapins will thrive.

ALTERNATIVE ACCOMMODATION

Although this chapter has been primarily concerned with keeping terrapins in fish-tanks, there are other ways of housing them. For example, in a pool in a greenhouse, or in an outdoor pond.

All you have to remember is to make your terrapin/s environment as much like its natural habitat as is possible. (See Chapter 2), i.e. your terrapin/s must have a constantly high temperature, adequate lighting, land on which to bask and sufficient swimming water. The equipment you will need, heating units, filters etc. can be bought from a garden centre specifically for ponds.

There are advantages especially in keeping the larger sizes of terrapin in greenhouses. The chelonians have a larger land area on which to walk and bask. Also possibly a greater depth of swimming water. A disadvantage with fish-tanks is that you have a limited space to create a terrapin-like environment. Also it is sometimes difficult to incorporate a three or four foot tank into the average home.

However, as well as advantages there are also disadvantages. The first thing that springs to mind is that the terrapins must have either a source of artificial light in the greenhouse of garden shed, or a teaspoon of cod or halibut liver oil at least once a week. The reason for this is that as natural sunlight passes through glass, the higher frequencies, notably ultra-violet rays, are filtered out. As a result the terrapin is unable to extract vitamin D, which is needed to work with calcium to give a strong shell. Lack of Vitamin D causes a nasty disease called Soft-Shell. This will be gone into in a later chapter. There could also be the problems with insects and fungus. Regular checks on your terrapins should be made to ensure their health.

In this country the hardier species of terrapin (for example, the European Pond Terrapin) are best housed in outdoor ponds only during the warm summer weather. In winter it is necessary to house them indoors.

Chapter 4

BUYING A TERRAPIN

HAVE THE TANK READY

The time to buy your terrapin is only when you have a tank completely set up and ready for it. The terrapin must be put into a heated tank straightaway, otherwise its growth may be affected later, especially in the case of hatchlings.

SELECTION

Do not be in a rush to buy the first terrapin you see, look around and obtain the healthiest. Observe to see what conditions the terrapins have been kept in. The ones in the roomy, heated and lighted tanks with rocks and shallow water are the healthiest ones to buy. The terrapins kept in cold, dark and small overcrowded conditions are likely to be unhealthy and some may be dying. However, it is surprising how some recover completely when put into a nice warm tank. But remember, a sick terrapin is extremely difficult to cure and will only cause upset later. Look for a terrapin which is bright-eyed, alert and active. Look for one with a good shell, i.e.; no abrasions on it or breaks. Ask the assistant if he or she will get out the terrapin from its tank for you to check. Now very gently touch the area of the shell just before the tail. If it visibly bends do not buy it. This terrapin is likely to have a disease called **Soft Shell**. The disease is very hard to cure in a hatchling. If, however, the shell is firm and you are happy with the terrapin then buy it. Here I would like to say that it is hard to tell what sex hatchlings are. Do not go to buy wanting a male and a female — it is the luck of the draw as to what you actually get. A terrapin with a carapace length of 2½ inches and over can be sexed. See Chapter 8 on breeding for the differences between male and female. After buying your terrapin get it home as quickly as possible and put it into the tank.

NUMBER TO KEEP

A word about how many terrapins to buy. Do not be silly and get three or four. Terrapins grow very quickly and it will mean buying another tank and equipment, or finding homes for some of them later. I know that finding homes for terrapins is a difficult job. The ideal number to keep is two. Be sure that you know what species of terrapin you have bought. I have heard of people going out to buy a 'Red-Eared' terrapin, and have come back with Snapping terrapins. Some species of terrapin like the Snapping varieties are more difficult and dangerous to keep, than the average N.American varieties, i.e., Red-Eared, Map and Painted terrapins. Be sure that the terrapin you want is the one you buy.

I would like to say that if you buy a hatchling it is prone to disease because of its size and immaturity. Hatchlings have a high mortality rate and need more attention than the mature terrapins. However, if kept in a suitably equipped tank it has every chance of growing and living healthily. An adult terrapin is hardier but will require a larger tank, more food and will cost more to buy.

Finally, a terrapin should be supported with your hand underneath its plastron. Never hold a terrapin tightly at the sides, this could damage a hatchling's shell.

The size and variety of terrapin that you buy is your decision, just remember all that has been stated. In the next chapter the terrapin's diet will be discussed.

Chapter 5

NUTRITION AND FEEDING

BALANCED DIET ESSENTIAL

To keep terrapins successfully, apart from the suitable tank environment required, these reptiles must have a balanced diet. A balanced diet contains all the essential nutrients, minerals and vitamins which a terrapin needs for growth, bone and shell formation and repair of damaged tissue. Terrapins are mainly carnivores, but besides the meat, fish and seafood they need a small amount of fruit and vegetable matter in their diet for it to be balanced.

Meat contains protein, a little fat and some minerals and vitamins. Fish contains protein, calcium in the bones, and fat and vitamins A and D in the fish liver oils. Shrimp and other forms of seafood contain a high percentage of protein. Protein is the nutrient required for growth and repair of cells. Not only internal cells, but the terrapins' scales and nails also need protein.

Protein
Although calcium is present in fish bones, the hatchlings particularly, should also be given cuttlefish bone or natural chalk which are excellent sources of this mineral. Calcium in conjunction with vitamin D is responsible for bone and shell formation. Hatchlings need more calcium than adults because their shells are immature. In the first year of life calcium is laid down in the bones and shells thus forming a strong, supportive structure. In the hatchlings early years calcium is required for the shells to grow. A fully grown

adult however requires only enough calcium to keep its bones and shell strong and healthy. A diet deficient in either calcium, vitamin D or both will result in **Soft Shell**. This is a disease similar to rickets in humans, and it is very difficult to cure. This disease is partly responsible for the high mortality rate in hatchlings. Vitamin D is present not only in fish liver oils, but also in natural and artificial sunlight. Also the oils help to lubricate the terrapin's digestive tract thus preventing constipation. Surprisingly this is a common ailment in reptiles. Oils are grouped under fats which are excellent nutrients in that they contain more energy per gram than either proteins or carbohydrates.

Fruit and Vegetables

The other part of a terrapin's diet should consist of a small amount of fruit and vegetable matter. These foods contain important minerals and vitamins which are not present in carnivorous foods. For example, vitamin A in tomato and carrot; the B vitamins in green vegetables; and vitamin C in banana and orange. Vegetable foods are high in fibre (roughage) again good in preventing constipation. The B vitamins help to keep the nervous system functioning properly. A diet deficient in them could result in **Avitaminosis B**. Brown wholemeal bread also contains these vitamins. If your terrapins will not eat fruit or vegetable foods, they should be given a condition tablet to obtain the necessary vitamins and minerals.

DIET TABLE

To recap what has been said, overleaf is a table showing what should be included in a terrapin's diet, along with the nutrients and minerals and vitamins which the foods contain.

FOOD	NUTRIENTS	MINERALS	VITAMINS
Meat	Fat Protein	Magnesium Iron (Liver & Kidney only)	$(B_1\ B_2\ B_{12})$ (Liver only)
Fish	Fat Protein	Magnesium Calcium Phosphorous Iodine	A D (Liver oils)
Cuttlefish Bone Natural Chalk		Calcium Phosphorus	
Seafood	Protein	Sodium Chlorine (as chloride)	
Fruit	Mainly Carbohydrate	Potassium	A C
Vegetable	Mainly Carbohydrate	Iron	A, B_1, B_2, C
Bread	Mainly Carbohydrate		B_1

SPECIAL POINTS

When you have just bought your terrapin there is the possibility that it will be reluctant to eat. Tempt it with live foods such as tubifex works or daphnia; these live foods wriggle and jump and this will stimulate the hatchling to eat. For the first few days feed the terrapin on this type of food. When it has settled down in its new environment follow the diet below.

Hatchlings should be fed on small pieces of cat meat; e.g. **Whiskas**. Alternate this with fish (sardines in oil/herring or sprats, etc.) and shrimp; e.g. **Pacific** shrimp. Cuttlefish bone can either be sprinkled on the food or small pieces about the size of ½p's can be put into the tank. Hatchlings should be given a little water cress, also small pieces of fruit; if your terrapins will eat brown bread then feed them this. Crush up a **Tibs** cat condition tablet and put onto the food twice weekly, also give a teaspoon of halibut or cod-liver oil once a week.

Adults should be given exactly the same foods, but obviously in larger quantities. Also they prefer the bigger varieties of shrimp. It is not necessary to give a fully grown adult terrapin cuttlefish bone, because calcium is present in the fish bones. After cooking herring, remove the bones because these are hard to digest and could choke a terrapin. However, the bones of other fish such as sardines and sprats are softer and should be fed to the terrapins. Adults should be given a **Tibs** condition tablet once a week.

A table to show the frequency of feeding, for a two month old hatchling to an adult terrapin of four years and over is given below:

AGE	FREQUENCY
2 months	Twice daily (e.g. 9am/9pm)
3 months	Daily
6 months	4 times weekly
3 years	3 times weekly
4 years & older	2 times weekly

HOW TO FEED

Now you know what the correct foods are to feed your terrapins, the next step is how to feed it.

All you need is a reasonable sized bowl. A washing-up bowl is as good as any. Put a shallow level of luke-warm water in it. Place the bowl on a towel on a table. It may be necessary to have a desk lamp shining onto the water if in a dark area of the room. Feed one terrapin at a time. All you do is put a square of food into the bowl and get the terrapin to eat it. It will soon learn, later on it will take food from your fingers. The water is vital as terrapins do not seem to be able to eat without it. One theory is that they do not produce saliva, so the water is required to lubricate their throats to form a bolus of food which can be swallowed. After the terrapin has eaten enough, put him back into the tank and get out another to feed.

The reason for feeding your terrapins in a separate bowl, not in the tank is for health reasons. No filter is powerful or efficient enough to clean away food particles as well as faeces and skin which is always being cast off. If you want a reasonably clean tank do not feed your terrapins in it.

If your terrapins are given a correct diet they will be strong, healthy and happy. To finish off this chapter I would like to say that any *Freeze-dried* food such as ant-eggs, tubifex worms, daphnia or dried insects are *not* the correct foods to feed to your terrapins. They contain little or nothing of nutritional value.

GRAVEL

After feeding your terrapins, you may notice that on returning to their tank they immediately bite and swallow gravel, which covers the floor of the tank. The reason for this is purely instinctive. The gravel passes into the terrapins gizzard (the part of the alimentary canal that follows the stomach). Due to the movements of the muscular lining, the gravel is mixed up with the food particles and grinds them into smaller particles which enzymes (biological catalysts) can work on, in the process of digestion. In humans the molars (grinding teeth) grind the food we eat into a size so small that the stomach enzymes can work on it, to begin the process of digestion, absorption and assimilation. Terrapins do not have teeth — only a beak. They can bite off food but cannot grind it up in their mouths to a small size for digestion to take place. The gravel is taking the part of the molar teeth and also primary enzymes.

The gravel eating is nothing to do with the terrapin being so hungry that it will eat anything. Neither does it indicate that the terrapin is deficient of some vital mineral or vitamin in its diet.

Chapter 6

GROWTH

A hatchling that is fed on a well-balanced, nutritious diet is likely to grow into a strong, healthy adult. This part of the book deals with the rate of growth of a hatchling and its 'plate' shedding. To start with I have composed a table showing growth in the Red-Eared Terrapin.

Table to show the rate of growth in both male and female

Male	One month to one year growth of carapace		One to two years growth of carapace		Two to five years growth of carapace
	Inches	Cms	Inches	Cms	
Jan	1¼	3.2	4	10.2	In the next three
Feb	1½	3.8	4	10.2	years the male
March	1¾	4.4	4	10.2	grew 1½ inches
April	2.1	5.3	4¼	10.8	(3.8 cms). He
May	2¼	5.7	4¼	10.8	therefore had a
June	2½	6.4	4½	11.4	fully grown
July	2¾	7.0	4½	11.4	carapace length
August	3.1	7.9	4.8	12.2	of 6½ inches
Sept.	3¼	8.3	4.8	12.2	(16.5 cms)
Oct.	3½	8.9	4.8	12.2	
Nov.	3¾	9.5	4.8	12.2	
Dec.	4	10.2	5	12.7	

Female	The rate of growth is slightly faster i.e. by December the female's carapace length was 4½ inches (11.4cms)	The second phase of growth is also quicker. The 2 year old female measured 7 inches (17.8cms)	Here the rate of growth is identical to the males. i.e. 1½ inches (3.8) in 3 years. The full carapace length was 8½ inches (21.6cms)

The width of the carapace is generally one inch (2.5cms) less than the length.

The growth chart shows the growth of a captive male and female over a period of five years. Five years is the age at which a terrapin is fully grown. After five years of age a terrapin is still growing, but so slowly that the figures can not be recorded. Example, one centimetre a year or less. The chart shows growth of the 'Red-Eared' terrapin only.

RATE OF GROWTH

A male terrapin grows quickly from the age of one month to one year. As can be seen from the chart it grows approximately ¼ inch a month. From one to two years, the rate slows down to about ¼ inch every three months. From two to five years the terrapin is still growing, but very slowly.

At the age of five a terrapin can be considered fully grown, although they are classed as adults upon sexual maturity at three years of age.

Female growth

A female terrapin follows almost the same growth pattern as a male from the ages of one month to one year. However from one to two years it grows at a rate of ¼ inch every two months. The rate of growth from two to five years is the same as for a male. Females are usually at least two inches longer in carapace length than the male.

Stages

As a terrapin gets bigger, its skin no longer fits, so it is cast off. The old skin around the head, neck, limbs and tail are shed first. It is easy to see this when the terrapin is in water. The new skin is a brighter colour. When the shells grow, what I refer to as 'plates' come off.

Diagram of the carapace and plastron. The diagrams were drawn by the author using a female Red-Eared terrapin as her model.

CARAPACE

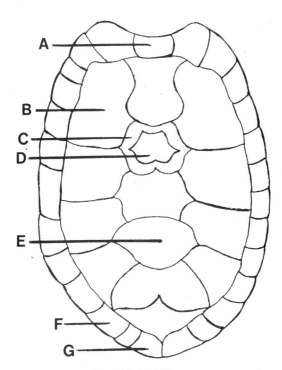

KEY FOR CARAPACE
A – Nuchal Plate
B – Costal Plate
C – New plate grows underneath old plate
D – Old plate ready for shedding
E – Vertebral Plate
F – Marginal Plate
G – Supracaudal Plate

Diagram of the Plastron, drawn by the author using a female Red-Eared terrapin as her model.

PLASTRON

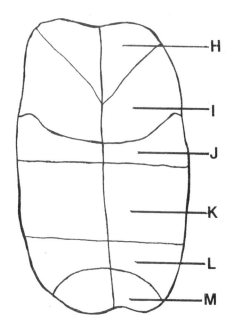

KEY FOR PLASTRON
H – Interegular Plate
I – Humeral
J – Pectoral
K – Abdominal
L – Femoral
M – Anal Plate

LET THE PLATES FALL OFF

The old plates when almost ready for coming off are like bits of cellotape. DO NOT PULL THEM OFF. If they are pulled off, they will also remove part of the new delicate plate underneath; therefore the terrapin is left with a permanent grey discoloured area. The new plate underneath is composed of very delicate cells and therefore the top plate needs to be completely dead, before it comes away. It will do so in its own time. The older a terrapin is, the more 'growth rings' it has.

**PHOTOGRAPHS SHOWING
ACTUAL PLATES FROM THE
RED-EARED TERRAPIN**

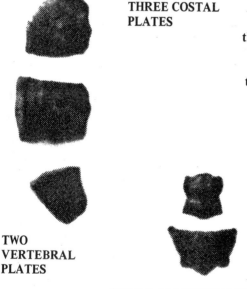

**THREE COSTAL
PLATES**

As terrapins grow, they do sometimes knock themselves against rocks in boisterous play and mark their shells. As they are rough and fun-loving it would be impossible for a terrapin to reach the age of five without some scratch or mark on its shell.

**TWO
VERTEBRAL
PLATES**

SHELL MAINTENANCE

To keep the shell looking attractive and healthy when the terrapins are exercised rub a little halibut/cod liver oil or olive oil into their carapace.

Chapter 7

EXERCISE

WALKING IS GOOD FOR THEM

Earlier on, I mentioned that terrapins are as well adapted to land as they are to water. They not only like to bask on rocks in the sun, but enjoy roaming about exploring their terrestrial environment. Also, walking develops different muscles in their legs to what are normally used for swimming.

It must be remembered that most imported terrapins are tropical varieties. Therefore it is only on very warm days that they can be put outside for exercise. If the terrapin is put in a small enclosed space it will get very little exercise; but if given the area of the whole garden, will run all over the place. It is very important to watch them all the time — terrapins are easy to lose. They blend in well with the plants and grass. Also, do not exercise too many terrapins at once. You will find watching a couple is hard enough. On letting them go free in the grass you will be amazed at their speed. Unlike tortoises, terrapins can run. It does not matter what size your terrapin is. Obviously the big ones will need more exercise than the small ones. Do not let an ill or unhealthy terrapin out; it will more than likely be-come worse as it may pick up further infections in the garden. In a year there are few days when the terrapins can enjoy ten minutes in the garden. In winter, exercise your terrapins on a carpetted floor for about five minutes daily. I think that walking is an extremely beneficial exercise for them and is a change from their tank. You will find that terrapins enjoy climbing over things — be it you or an object on the floor. These reptiles have no sense of danger, so you really have to watch them all the time. If your terrapin falls onto its back put it the right way up straight away. A tortoise or terrapin on its back will not survive for long.

DANGERS

Two further things to mention are concerned with digging and temperature. Do not let any terrapin bury itself either in soil or grass because they are very difficult to find, as I have already mentioned. The only time a terrapin is allowed to dig, is in the case of a mature female who is going to lay eggs. As for temperature, do not keep your captive terrapins in the sun for more than a few minutes. You will find they will make a bee-line for trees and small plants where there is some shade. If terrapins are left in the sun's direct path for long, it may kill them.

Finally, after the terrapins have been exercised, put them in a plastic bowl of luke-warm water and clean all the soil and grass off them. I am convinced that walking is an essential exercise that keeps terrapins fit, strong and healthy.

EXERCISE AREA

Regular exercise outside the tank or pond is essential. An area in the garden or even a small movable pen may be used. Alternatively, a building may be adapted for exercising and, carried to the ultimate, an environmental chamber may be created where hatching and rearing can be carried out under controlled conditions.

Chapter 8

BREEDING

For the three following chapters I am using the 'Red-Eared' terrapin as an example. This is because I have bred this variety of terrapin myself.

SEXING

The earliest one can try to tell whether a terrapin is male or female, is at approximately seven months of age when the carapace length should be 2¾ to 3¼ inches. Obviously adult terrapins are easy to distinguish between, because of their size and maturity.

I have listed the differences between a 'Red-Eared' male and female below.

MALE	FEMALE
1. Bright red stripe behind each eye.	Dull orangy-brown stripe behind each eye.
2. Exaggerated foreclaws (length 2¼ cms)	Shorter foreclaws (length 1 cm)
3. Male is quite small compared with the female; e.g. 6½ inches carapace length when adult; i.e. three years old.	Female is much bigger and heavier than the male; e.g. 8½ inches carapace length when adult.
4. Long, thick tail (very thick at the base).	Shorter and more slender tail

Diagram of a Tail (Male)	Diagram of a Tail (Female)

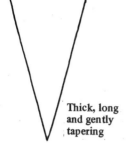 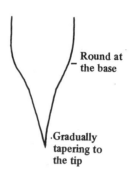

Thick, long and gently tapering

Round at the base

·Gradually tapering to the tip

5. Plastron curves up towards the rear end.

Flat plastron at the rear end.

Diagram of Plastron

Diagram of Plastron

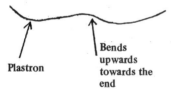 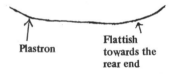

Plastron

Bends upwards towards the end

Plastron

Flattish towards the rear end

6. On the whole, the male has a slender, narrow body.

Bigger build and thickset (the skeletal frame is modified for egg laying giving a heavier and wider frame).

Apart from points one and two, the differences can be applied to any variety of terrapin. Also the size will be different in other species.

REPRODUCTION

Sexual reproduction in all terrapins and turtles takes place in water. However, the resulting eggs are laid on land. Now I would like to say a bit about the basic principles of reproduction. The male terrapin produces a large quantity of **sperm**, whereas the female only produces a small amount of **ova**. The sperm and ova are **sex cells** or **gametes**. They both contain only half the genetic material found in all other living cells. When the two halves meet; i.e. a sperm and ovum cell, a cell with the full compliment of genetic material or D.N.A. (deoxyribonucleic acid) is produced. This cell multiplies and eventually becomes an embryo. The embryo grows as it feeds off the yolk in the egg and eventually emerges as a hatchling, usually about eight to twelve weeks after the egg was laid.

THE ADULT TERRAPIN

When a terrapin is three years old it is classed as an adult. Providing it is fit and healthy, and is fully grown there is no reason why it should not be fertile. If you have a mature adult male and female, providing they have plenty of room in their tank they should mate. The water level should be at least six inches deep, and one third of the tank should be land. The tank should be at least 3ft x 1ft x 15 inches. I would like to say that eggs will *not* be produced after just one mating. It may take two years of doing so, before the female lays any eggs. Usually the first four or five eggs are laid in the tank one by one. **These are almost always infertile**. It is only the clutches of eggs that the female buries that are fertile. An average clutch contains four eggs.

COURTSHIP AND MATING

I shall now go through the stages of courtship, copulation and mating in the 'Red-Eared' terrapin.

Courtship

Firstly, courtship in this variety of terrapin may go on for six months or more before any mating takes place. The first noticeable sign is that the little male keeps sniffing the back-end of the female in the way dogs sniff each other. **This is shown in drawing below.**

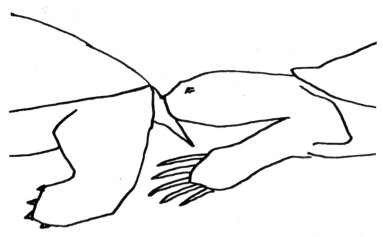

Drawing I

Next the male tries to get the female's attention. This he does by swimming around her continuously, and also by snapping at her. During courtship the poor female may be bitten quite frequently on and around her neck and throat. After five to ten minutes the male vibrates his long exaggerated foreclaws in the female's face. She responds by biting them. It is not surprising, as the claws catch on her eyes and nostrils!

Drawing II shows the male vibrating his long claws in the female's face.

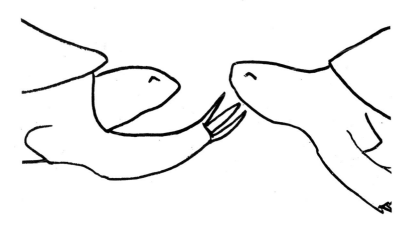

Mating

At this point the male darts to the back of the female, and begins to mount her. If the female is not in approval she will swing round and the male falls off. If however, she appears not to mind, she will remain still. The little male takes time to get right on top of her so that he can reach her neck with his mouth.

Copulation is a difficult affair – the male has to be perfectly balanced. To do this he relies on the female co-operating. Finally as quick as a flash the male positions his tail over the female's and then bites the back of her neck (simply to hang on during transfer of the sperm). Together they frantically swim in this position around the tank, hitting and bumping into objects. The whole process is a very violent matter and is very noisy.

Mating only takes two or three minutes, so it is chance whether the male manages to transfer his sperm to the female. The female can store sperm until she has ova to fertilise. All the stages of reproduction; i.e. courtship, copulation and mating, may take up to an hour depending upon how much the female is willing to co-operate.

Photographs III and IV show the male mounting the female.

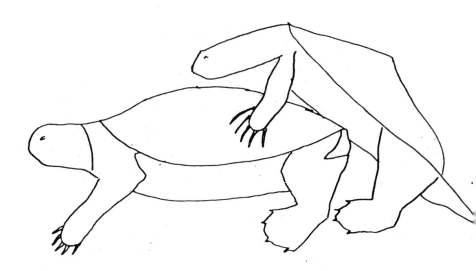

Drawing III — Here the male has just started to mount his chosen female.

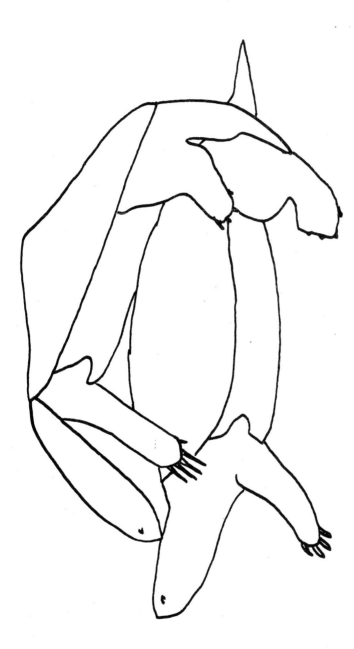

Drawing IV —
In this final drawing the male is just about to bite the female's neck before sexual reproduction.

CHAPTER 9

LAYING THE EGGS

CARRYING THE EGGS

As previously mentioned the female now stores the sperm until she has ova to fertilise. After fertilisation, the fertilised ova are each deposited in an egg shell with a vast quantity of pale yellow, oily yolk. The yolk is the embryo's food supply until hatching; which on average is nine weeks later.

The skeletal frame of the female Red-Eared terrapin is modified so as to allow her to both carry and lay the eggs. It is the pelvic area which is modified, the bones termed the "pubic symphasis" are not fused. This allows the eggs to be passed through the remaining gap to be laid. A female can carry as many as eight large eggs at any one time.

GETTING READY TO LAY

It is easy to recognise a female who has eggs to lay. There are three main signs which she displays that would be difficult to miss.

Firstly, and most noticeably, she tries (and may succeed) to get out of the tank. This she does by standing on her hindlegs and concentrates all her weight against the lid. You will find it is necessary to have large, heavy books on top of the lid, along its entire length, or some other method of securing the top. A female in an egg laying condition is a real 'heavy-weight', and will try almost anything to get out of the tank. The reason for preventing her getting out is simply so she does not damage either herself or her eggs in falling. However, the female must be put outside in the garden for at least half an hour every day to give her a chance to lay the eggs. It is essential that she is watched all the time, otherwise she may get lost under a hedge or bush.

The second sign that she will undoubtably display is digging. If put onto a surface out of the tank she will try to dig a hole in it, with her hindlegs.

Finally, she may be reluctant to eat until her eggs are laid. These signs may go on for weeks until she finds a suitable place to lay.

On finding a suitable spot she will start to dig a hole. To do this the female uses her large webbed hindlegs. With her claws she scrapes away soil and deposits this on either side of the hole.

Photograph I, below, shows a female Red-Eared terrapin digging a hole in sandy soil. Note the soil in her left foot which she has scraped away from the inside of the hole.

Photograph I

It took the female in the picture approximately an hour to dig the hole.

The **Second photograph shows** the female with her right hindleg in the now, deep hole. She is in the process of scraping away more soil to deepen the hole even more. The time taken for a female to dig a hole varies, depending on the type of soil and how quickly the terrapin works; i.e. digging a hole in sandy soil is easier than digging one in a clay soil.

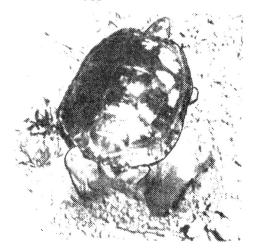

After the hole is completed the female now lays her eggs in it. As each egg is laid she carefully positions it in the hole with her hind feet. Egg laying only takes about five to ten minutes, the number of eggs laid varies. The terrapin pictured in the photographs on this occasion laid six large eggs and two vestigial ones (these contained no yolk). **Photographs III and IV** show the egg tube lengthening as an egg is about to be laid. Not the difference in length of the tube in the two photographs. With this in mind there was only less than half a minute between both pictures.

Photograph III

49

Photograph IV

Photograph V shows the egg
actually descending from
the egg-tube. Note the
female's right hindleg
which is getting ready to
position the egg in the
hole.

Photograph V

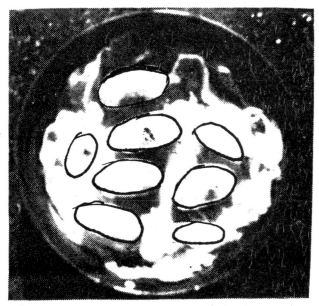

Finally, **Photograph VI** shows a shallow tray lined with damp paper-towels. On the paper towels are six large, fertile eggs and two very much smaller ones. The final picture was taken five minutes after the last egg was laid.

PROCEDURE AFTER LAYING

When you are sure that your female has laid all her eggs, put her onto another patch of soil nearby. Now very carefully start to retrieve the eggs she has laid. DO NOT TURN them because this will kill the embryos inside the eggs. Put them all on a shallow tray lined with damp paper-towels; i.e. kitchen towels. This is so they do not dry out; however, the slime on the outside of the eggs hardens to give a protective outer covering.

The diagram below shows a longitudinal section through a Red-Eared terrapin's egg chamber.

EGG CHAMBER DIAGRAM

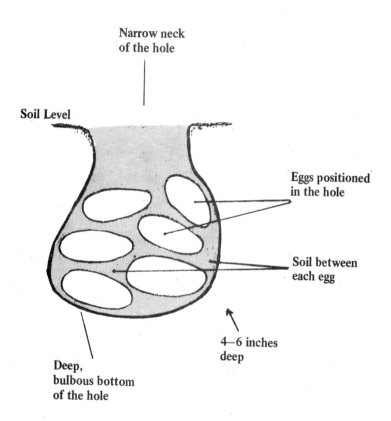

Narrow neck
of the hole

Soil Level

Eggs positioned
in the hole

Soil between
each egg

4–6 inches
deep

Deep,
bulbous bottom
of the hole

FINAL CHECKING

Before putting the female back in the tank, wash all the soil off her in a bowl of luke-warm water. Also check that she has no cuts. Chapter 10 deals with incubating the eggs.

Red-Eared Terrapin

Chapter 10

INCUBATING THE EGGS

INCUBATION

For domesticated birds such as poultry the practice of incubation by machine is well established and incubators are now capable of producing very good results. In the reptile world artificial incubation is still in its infancy and, therefore, the would-be breeder of terrapins must be prepared for disappointments.

The essentials are:

1. Heat

2. Moisture for humidity

3. Patience

There is no question of trying to achieve a constantly stable temperature. It will be appreciated that, unlike bird incubation, there is no body warmth to keep the eggs at a steady temperature so fluctuations occur in the natural state.

TRAYING

After removing the eggs from the hole, place them on a shallow tray lined with damp paper towels (see Chapter 9, last paragraph). Take them inside and gently wash off any soil from the shells. Take care not to turn them while doing this, also DO NOT WASH OFF THE SLIME – this later hardens giving a protective covering to the egg. Handling the eggs is tricky because of their sliminess, and because they are heavy with fluid and yolk. After the eggs have been dried, place in the same shallow dish on a damp paper towel.

Fill the spaces between each egg with strips of damp paper towels, so that the eggs do not touch and their sides are moist. Next place a damp paper towel over the top of all the eggs.

THE INCUBATOR

Put the dish in a clean biscuit tin – this provides the eggs with a good humid climate. My experience with a plastic container has not been successful; it made the eggs dry out and was too hot an environment for the embryos to survive but other people have been quite successful with plastic boxes. Put the tin at the back of an airing cupboard. The tin's temperature should be approximately 80 to 85 degrees fahrenheit. The eggs should hatch between eight and twelve weeks.

An alternative approach to the procedure described above is to use a small chick incubator with the temperature control modified to the mid-point temperature of 82.5ºF. The exact temperature would be set after experience with the first hatch. Remember that the temperature level is not as critical as for chicks.

PROCEDURES WITH DIY INCUBATORS

It is necessary to check the eggs about twice a week. The method described above is good in that you can see what is happening; i.e. if any eggs go mouldy or bad you can re-move them, thus preventing further spreading onto good eggs. The one bad point with the home-made incubation method is that it allows mould to grow. This should be scraped away, twice weekly. Any mouldy paper towels are best completely removed and replaced with good ones.

After two weeks if any paper towels need replacing, then do so — but do not wet their replacements. The outsides of the eggs should now be hard and do not need to be kept moist as much. Do not wet the top paper towel, but on top of this put a damp one. The idea of this is so the other towels will gradually be dampened; but because the eggs are not directly touching any very damp towels they will not grow mould. Now it will only be necessary to check the eggs, and dampen the very top paper towel once a week. Remember if the eggs need to be touched DO NOT TURN THEM and HANDLE CAREFULLY. Unless any eggs smell bad or are completely mouldy do not remove from the container. I have removed what I thought were bad eggs, but on opening have found them to be all right internally. The outer egg shell is very resistant and will be able to cope with a little mould etc.

If after a period (maximum twenty weeks) the eggs have not hatched, then it is unlikely they will do so. Between eight and twelve weeks is the usual time for eggs to hatch.

Below I have listed reasons why eggs do not hatch:—

1. Eggs were infertile.

2. Embryos were damaged when being transferred from the egg chamber to your dish.

3. Temperature in the airing cupboard was too cold, or more likely, too hot.

4. Eggs will dry out completely if damp paper towels are not put on and around them.

5. Mould may get into the eggs if not removed (or bacteria and tiny worms may do so if not washed off after the transfer). Some worm eggs can remain on the shell and hatch whilst in the airing cupboard. This is why

you should check the eggs regularly.

Hatching terrapin eggs is a very difficult and slow job. It is not easy and the eggs require plenty of attention. If you are lucky enough to hatch out terrapins, you will notice the young have a 'tooth' on the area just below their noses. It is a horny projection called the 'egg-tooth' which is used to cut the leathery shell on hatching. It drops off after one to two weeks. Also you will notice that the hatchlings have a bulbous attachment under their plastrons. This is the remains of the yolk sac. Over the first week it reduces in volume and is completely absorbed back into the terrapin. During this time the young will not eat, their nourishment is provided by the yolk sac. The hatchlings are very delicate so be careful when handling them. Their tank set up is the one for hatchlings described in Chapter 3. Details of their nutritional needs can be found in Chapter 5. When hatched the young are 1¼ inches in length (carapace length). Remember, do *not* put them in a tank with the parent terrapins, as they will be attacked and most likely killed.

OTHER METHODS

The method for hatching eggs can be used for all varieites of terrapin. To conclude I will say that there are other ways of incubating terrapin eggs. The method described, is the one I have found to be the easiest and most effective. It is the one I have personally had most success with. However, the mould problem presents difficulties and for this reason the use of **Vermiculite** is now becoming widespread. This is available as a roof insulation material. The chips are "mixed" with water to give the desired humidity and mould does not develop.

Chapter 11

VETERINARY SECTION

In this chapter I shall endeavour to describe some of the health problems that most commonly occur in terrapins, giving the symptoms and treatments. The illnesses are segregated into three different sections. To start with, the minor ailments are considered.

MINOR AILMENTS

1.CUTS, SCRATCHES and ABRASIONS
Treatment
Clean the wound with MILD antiseptic, e.g. T.C.P. (one capful to one pint of water). Swab the wound daily until a scab forms. Water used to dilute should be luke-warm. If the wound is deep and bleeding profusely, apply pressure to it and take to a veterinary surgeon.

2.CONSTIPATION
Symptoms
The terrapin passes black, tarry bowel movements. It is very noticeable that he has difficulty doing so.

Treatment
Give ½ teaspoon of liquid paraffin mixed into the food. (½ teasp. is the dose for an adult, give ¼ teasp. to a hatchling). This should be given twice weekly until the complaint subsides. Also, give very greasy, oily fish on a more regular basis; e.g. sardines in oil.

3.EYE INFECTIONS
Symptoms
An eye infection can appear to be like a red membrane covering the eye. It can literally appear overnight, or the terrapin can have just what looks to be a sore eye.

Treatment
Make up a bowl of weak saline solution, (to a bowl of water add two to three teasp. of common salt). Place the terrapin in the bowl and make sure the infected eye goes under water. You may find the terrapin will swim underwater. If it won't hold it under for a FEW SECONDS ONLY every so often. Do this for a duration of five minutes morning and night, until the infection has gone. After the problem has cleared up it is a good idea to put one teasp. of common salt into the tank water every week. This guards against further eye infections.

4.DAMAGED SHELL
Treat as in 1. If the break is big enough to reveal the terrapins flesh seek veterinary advice. Some breaks can be covered with plaster.

The second section deals with deficiency diseases and fungus.

DISEASES

1. SOFT SHELL
Stages of the disease and symptoms
First of all it is necessary to ascertain what stage of the disease your terrapin has. In Stage I the small plates just above the tail are soft. They bend slightly, this is common in hatchlings.

In Stage II, the terrapin does not eat much. It

SOFT-SHELL (Continued)

appears sluggish and its shell is soft from the middle to the back end. It bends easily when gently depressed. In the final stage the terrapin will not eat. It is too weak to move and it's shell is completely soft. You will be unable to hold it because of the risk of crushing it. To remove it from the tank place a support under its plastron. DO NOT LIFT THE SHELL FROM ABOVE it will break. In this **final stage** the hatchlings especially, make feeble crying, whistling noises as they open and shut their beaks. A terrapin can take up to a month to die after reaching this stage. Take it to a vets and have it put to sleep humanely.

The first stage is curable, the second is with lots of patience. The final stage is not usually curable.
Before giving the treatment for this disease it is necessary to understand just what soft-shell is and how to prevent it.

Soft-shell is a disease similar to rickets in man. It is often seen in hatchlings rather than the fully grown adults. The reason for this is because hatchlings need a greater quantity of calcium and vitamin D to make their bones and shells (carapace and plastron) strong, as they are growing. But adults who are fully grown only need enough of the minerals and vitamins to maintain the balance within the bones, shells and blood system.

As I have said before, soft-shell is a deficiency disease where the terrapin is deficient of vitamin D and calcium. Therefore to cure the disease the patient needs to be fed large quantities of nutrients which contain these necessary factors.

About Vitamin D and Calcium
Vitamin D is present in sunlight and artificial light to a lesser extent.

Soft-shell (Continued)

It is also present in fish liver oils i.e. halibut and cod liver oils. It has to be present for the absorption of calcium.
Calcium is a mineral which is needed for bone and shell formation. Good sources of calcium are as calcium carbonate (natural chalk) or cuttlefish bone. Cuttlefish bone is the buoyancy organ of the squid. It has a hard solid back with a thick, chalky layer on top of this. It is the chalky layer which is broken off and given to the terrapins to eat.

Treatment (Stage I)

Is your terrapin in a tank which is not heated? If so see Chapter 3 on setting up a tank suitable for hatchlings. One of the reasons for the disease is that the terrapin is living in cold conditions. The body temperature lowers so much that the terrapin will not eat. This leads to malnutrition and subsequently soft-shell. Once in a heated tank the treatment is easy. Your terrapin should start eating so put halibut or cod-liver oil on his catmeat. Also break off chunky, but small pieces of cuttlefish bone and place them in the tank. Most hatchlings cannot resist a bite. However, if your terrapin does not eat it sprinkle it on its food. When out of the tank rub halibut or cod liver oil into its shell – VERY GENTLY. Also take him outside if the weater is dry and warm. If not, place him under a desk lamp for five minutes twice a day. If all these things are done it is likely that your terrapin will be cured (see Chapter 5 on nutrition).

Treatment for Stage II

As the terrapin is not eating, or not eating much it is vital to get it eating properly. This is done by 'feeding' it nasogastrically. To do this fill a bowl with luke-warm water and into it sprinkle a fair amount of cuttlefish bone as well as a teaspoon of a food supplement, which can be obtained from a vets. Put the terrapin in the water and dip it for a few seconds only, underwater. Do this every so often for a duration of five minutes, twice daily. DO

Soft-shell (Continued)

NOT HOLD THE TERRAPIN UNDERWATER. For the few seconds that it goes underwater, particles of calcium and supplement will enter through its nose (make sure the cuttlefish bone and supplement are very well mixed into the water – not floating on the surface). For a terrapin that is not eating this is the only way to feed it. As it obtains the minerals and vitamins it will get stronger, and will want to eat. Do everything mentioned as for Stage I. Subject the terrapin to artificial or preferably real sunlight to absorb vitamin D from the rays. A terrapin with soft-shell in Stage II may or may not be cured. It is a painstakingly slow process, taking many months to bring about a full recovery. Curing soft-shell can be done, I have done so on a number of occasions using the above treatments.

2. AVITAMINOSIS B
This is a disease caused by lack of the B vitamins.

Symptoms
The terrapin walks slowly. As its limbs come down to reach the ground they are thrashed down, as if drunk. Its gait is unsteady and unco-ordinated. It keeps rotating its head from side to side and seems unable to stop. The terrapin eats less, till it gradually will not eat. It becomes weak and disinterested – the apparent drunken state gets worse.

Treatment
Obtain a nutritional supplement used for dogs or cats from your veterinary surgeon. This contains all the essential minerals and vitamins needed for healthy living, including the B vitamins. Give ¼ to ½ teaspoon of supplement daily (dose depends upon the size of terrapin). Feed nasogastrically as described for soft shell. Mix the

Avitaminosis B (Continued)

supplement in with the water well. Waft the particles in the direction of the terrapin's nose. Do this twice a day until your terrapin can eat properly. Then sprinkle the dose of supplement on its fish or meat at least twice a week. When the feed is used up just crush up a 'tibs' cat condition tablet and put this on the food once a week. Recovery is slow and the treatment can take up to a month, but persevere. It is easy to tell if your terrapin is making progress by assessing its walk every day.

3. FUNGUS

This is a parasitic or saprophytic member of the thallo-phytes (first group of plants including the algae). It starts as spores which germinate into hyphae (thread like growths). These can be picked up in a garden or borne in the air. The spores grow on the terrapin and the hyphae feed off it parasitically. This can eventually kill the host (terrapin). The problem is killing the fungus without killing the terrapin.

Symptoms

In water the fungi looks like cobwebs around the limbs and neck of the terrapin. It is not so easy to see when the reptile is on dry land. The terrapin eats less, becomes lethargic and slower in action.

Treatment

Some copper compounds can kill the fungus, example a preparation of copper sulphate from your vets. But if the fungi is profuse the terrapin is unlikely to recover. However, the copper sulphate should be added to the tank water. It is best to have a smaller plastic hospital tank, equipped with just a heating unit for problems like this one.

Finally, a problem which many terrapins have to put up

with is worms.

3. PARASITES
ECTOPARASITIC NEMOTODES
Origin
The eggs of these nemotodes are often found in sand or dirty gravel. If putting anything in your tank (especially rocks, sand and gravel) make sure it is clean. Sand can usually be bought sterilized from an aquarium. The problem starts when dirty of non-disinfected material is placed in the tank. A combination of heat, light and moisture have the effect of hatching out the nemotode eggs. Once this happens the worms make their way to the terrapins and feed off them. They tend to congregate on the glass sides of the tank, especially in corners around filters.

Symptoms
The visual evidence of worms is enough to tell you what the problem is. However until there are hundreds of them, they are not always easy to see. The terrapins appear off colour. If looked at closely you will see areas, example limbs, neck and especially tail which look to have been bitten. Also the terrapins may act strangely.

Below is a **diagram of an ectoparasitic nemotode.**

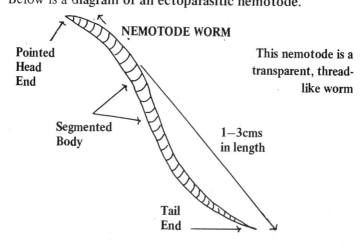

NEMOTODE WORM

Pointed Head End

This nemotode is a transparent, thread-like worm

Segmented Body

1–3cms in length

Tail End

Parasites — Ectoparasitic nemotodes (Continued)

The problem with ectoparasites is where to break the vicious circle.

Diagram of the life-cycle of nemotode worms.

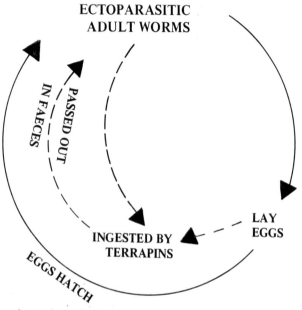

The dotted lines represent where the terrapins are involved. The problem is that if you get rid of the worms in the tank and even the remaining eggs, the terrapins re-infect the tank with worms in their faeces. These worms swim quite happily in the tank so it is not surprising that they get accidentally swallowed by the terrapins.

Treatment
The first type of treatment is to add a poison to the water which will kill the worms. A good one is STERAZIN which can be obtained from the Waterlife Re-

Parasites — Ectoparasitic nemotodes (Continued)

search Company, Heathrow, London. Follow the directions on the bottle and add the approximate number of drops. This is good if there are not so many worms in the tank. However, if there are thousands of worms, do the following:

Remove the terrapins from the tank — treat their wounds, bites, etc. as described in the first section of this chapter. Clean out the tank and all its equipment thoroughly using a strong disinfectant. Makes sure it is well rinsed out, however because it could be harmful to your terrapins. Also dry the tank completely. Put back all the equipment, etc.
Now you need a small plastic tank. You can buy a 1ft x 18inch tank very cheaply. Put the heating units in this tank and add the specified number of drops of sterazin to the water. Do not bother about building an area of land, but have the water fairly shallow. Everyday clean out this tank and add more sterazin, until the worms have apparently gone. The terrapins may need to be in the treatment tank for weeks before going back to their proper one. After two weeks of treatment the worms should have gone. However to make sure put water WITHOUT the sterazin in the tank for the terrapins. Do not change it, after a week, if there are no signs of worms all is well. Put the terrapins back in their tank. It would be as well to use the sterazin for another week, then stop using it.
If the terrapins are not eating, feed nasogastrically with a nutritional supplement, as described for soft-shell and avitaminosis B. To get rid of these worms it may take a long time, but the treatment usually works.

PREVENTION IS AIM

In conclusion I would like to say that sick terrapins as a rule are VERY difficult to treat. Usually terrapins with the illnesses mentioned will die. The secret in keeping terrapins is to make sure they have all the ingredients needed to make their lives healthy and happy. It is easier to prevent disease than it is to cure it.

Map Terrapin

TERRAPIN KEEPER'S CODE OF CONDUCT

1. Always wash hands after handling a terrapin.

2. Buy one pair of rubber gloves and one plastic washing up bowl. Keep for terrapin use only.

3. Always wear rubber gloves when putting your hands into the tank.

4. Always wash out the feeding bowl thoroughly after feeding your terrapins.

5. Clean the filter/s once a week to keep the tank looking and smelling pleasant.

6. The tank and all its equipment, rocks and gravel should be cleaned thoroughly at least once every six months.

If you keep to the 'Code of Conduct' you will get lots of pleasure from keeping terrapins. Hygiene is the all important word – REMEMBER IT.